GUITAR CHORDS

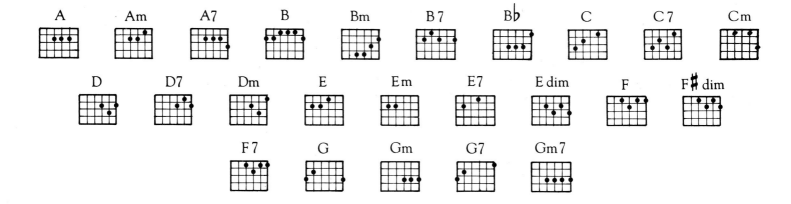

First published 1991 by
Pan Books Ltd,
Cavaye Place, London SW10 9PG

1 3 5 7 9 8 6 4 2

This collection © Pan Books Ltd 1991

Music setting © Lucy Duke 1991

ISBN 0 330 31490 4

Photoset by Rowland Phototypesetting Ltd
Bury St Edmunds, Suffolk

Printed and bound in Great Britain by
Springbourne Press Ltd, Basildon

Contents

Cockles and Mussels

1. In Dublin's fair ci – ty, where girls are so pret – ty, I first set my eyes on sweet

Mol – ly Malone, As she wheeled her wheelbarrow through streets broad and narrow, Crying,

CHORUS

'Cockles and mussels, a – live, a – live oh! A – live, a – live oh!__ A –

live, a – live oh!'__ Crying, 'Cockles and mus – sels, a – live, a – live oh!'

2. She was a fishmonger, but sure 'twas no wonder,
   For so were her father and mother before;
   And they each wheeled their barrow through streets broad and narrow,
   Crying, 'Cockles and mussels, alive, alive oh!'
   Chorus

3. She died of a fever, and no one could save her,
   And that was the end of sweet Molly Malone;
   Her ghost wheels her barrow through streets broad and narrow,
   Crying, 'Cockles and mussels, alive, alive oh!'
   Chorus

The Animals Went in Two by Two

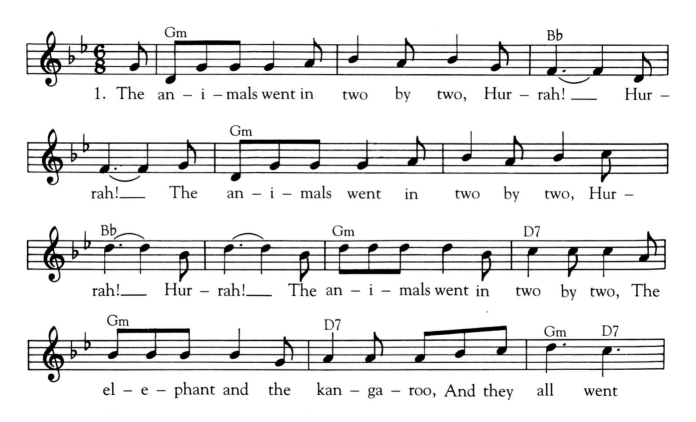

1. The an – i – mals went in two by two, Hur – rah! ___ Hur – rah! ___ The an – i – mals went in two by two, Hur – rah! ___ Hur – rah! ___ The an – i – mals went in two by two, The el – e – phant and the kan – ga – roo, And they all went

in – to the ark   For to get out of the rain.

2. The animals went in three by three . . .
   The wasp, the ant and the bumble bee . . .

3. The animals went in four by four . . .
   The great hippopotamus stuck in the door . . .

4. The animals went in five by five . . .
   By eating each other they kept alive . . .

5. The animals went in six by six . . .
   They turned out the monkey because of his tricks . . .

6. The animals went in seven by seven . . .
   The little pig thought he was going to heaven . . .

There's a Hole in my Bucket

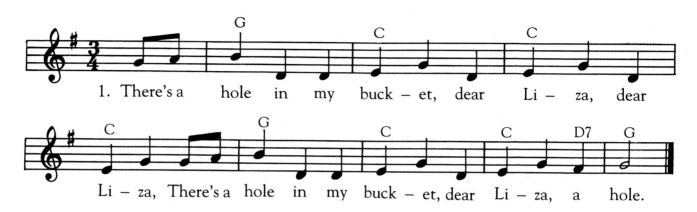

2. Then mend it, dear Henry, dear Henry, dear Henry,
   Then mend it, dear Henry, dear Henry, mend it!

3. With what shall I mend it, dear Liza? . . . with what?

4. With a straw, dear Henry . . . a straw!

5. But the straw is too long, dear Liza . . . too long.

8

6. Then cut it, dear Henry . . . cut it!

7. With what shall I cut it, dear Liza? . . . with what?

8. With a knife, dear Henry . . . a knife!

9. But the knife is too blunt, dear Liza . . . too blunt.

10. Then sharpen it, dear Henry . . . sharpen it!

11. With what shall I sharpen it, dear Liza? . . . with what?

12. With a stone, dear Henry . . . a stone!

13. But the stone is too dry, dear Liza . . . too dry.

14. Then wet it, dear Henry . . . wet it!

15. With what shall I wet it, dear Liza? . . . with what?

16. With water, dear Henry . . . with water!

17. In what shall I fetch it, dear Liza? . . . in what?

18. In a bucket, dear Henry . . . a bucket!

19. There's a hole in my bucket, dear Liza . . . a hole.

If You're Happy

1. If you're hap – py and you know it, clap your hands.   If you're

hap – py and you know it, clap your hands.   If you're happy and you know it, and you

real – ly want to show it,   If you're happy and you know it, clap your hands.

2. If you're happy and you know it,
   stamp your feet . . .

3. If you're happy and you know it,
   shout, 'We are' . . .

4. If you're happy and you know it,
   do all three . . .

A Sailor Went to Sea

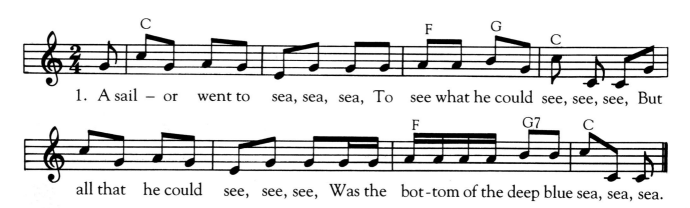

1. A sail – or went to sea, sea, sea, To see what he could see, see, see, But all that he could see, see, see, Was the bot-tom of the deep blue sea, sea, sea.

2. A sailor went to chop, chop, chop,
   To see what he could chop, chop, chop,
   But all that he could chop, chop, chop,
   Was the bottom of the deep blue chop, chop, chop.

12

3. A sailor went to knee, knee, knee,
   To see what he could knee, knee, knee . . .

4. A sailor went to toe, toe, toe,
   To see what he could toe, toe, toe . . .

5. A sailor went to heel, heel, heel,
   To see what he could heel, heel, heel . . .

6. A sailor went to sea, chop, knee, toe, heel,
   To see what he could see, chop, knee, toe, heel,
   But all that he could see, chop, knee, toe, heel,
   Was the bottom of the deep blue sea, chop, knee, toe, heel.

In the first verse, when you sing 'sea', touch your forehead with your right hand in time with the words. In the second verse, chop the crook of your arm as you sing 'chop', and in the remaining verses, touch the parts of the body mentioned in each. For the last verse, you must do *all* the actions.

She'll be Coming Round the Mountain

2. She'll be driving six white horses
   when she comes . . .

3. Oh, we'll all go out to meet her
   when she comes . . .

4. Oh, we'll kill the old red rooster
   when she comes . . .

5. And we'll all have chicken and dumplings
   when she comes . . .

6. Oh, she'll have to sleep with grandma
   when she comes . . .

7. She'll be wearing pink pyjamas
   when she comes . . .

Clementine

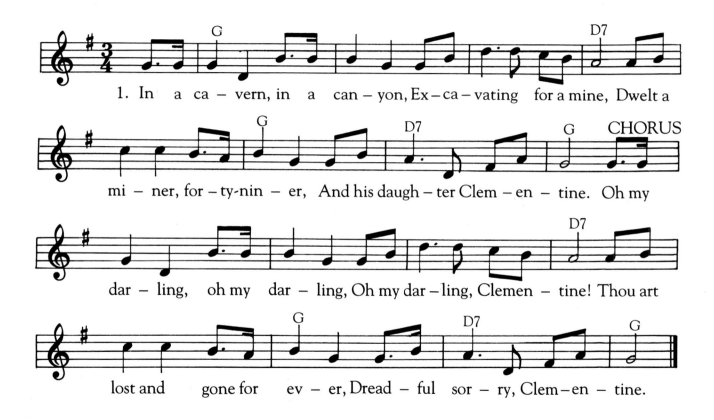

2. Light she was and like a fairy,
   And her shoes were number nine,
   Herring boxes without topses
   Sandals were for Clementine.
   Chorus

3. Drove she ducklings to the water
   Every morning just at nine.
   Hit her foot against a splinter,
   Fell into the foaming brine.
   Chorus

4. Saw her lips above the water
   Blowing bubbles mighty fine.
   But alas! I was no swimmer,
   So I lost my Clementine.
   Chorus

5. How I missed her, how I missed her,
   How I missed my Clementine.
   But I kissed her little sister
   And forgot my Clementine.
   Chorus

Polly-wolly-doodle

1. Oh! my Sal she am a__ maid–en fair, Singing 'Polly-wolly-doodle' all the day. With laugh – ing eyes and__ cur – ly hair, Sing 'Pol – ly-wol – ly-doodle' all the day.__ Fare thee well, fare thee well, Fare thee well, my fair – y fay, Oh, I'm off to Lou – isi – a – na For to

see my Su – sy An – na, Singing 'Pol – ly-Wol – ly-doo – dle' all the day.

2. Oh! a grasshopper sitting on a railroad track,
   Singing 'Polly-wolly-doodle' all the day,
   A-picking his teeth with a carpet tack,
   Sing 'Polly-wolly-doodle' all the day.

3. Behind a barn, down on my knees,
   Singing 'Polly-wolly-doodle' all the day,
   I thought I heard a chicken sneeze,
   Sing 'Polly-wolly-doodle' all the day.

4. He sneezed so hard with a whooping cough,
   Singing 'Polly-wolly-doodle' all the day,
   He sneezed his head and tail right off,
   Sing 'Polly-wolly-doodle' all the day.

Swing Low, Sweet Chariot

CHORUS

Swing low, sweet cha – ri – ot,___ Coming for to car – ry me home,

Swing low, sweet cha – ri – ot,___ Coming for to car – ry me home.

VERSE

1. I looked o – ver Jor – dan and what did I see,___

Com – ing for to car – ry me home? A band of an – gels

com — ing af — ter me,_____ Com — ing for to car — ry me home.

D.C.

2. If you get there before I do,
   Coming for to carry me home,
   Tell all my friends I'm coming too,
   Coming for to carry me home.
   Chorus

3. The brightest day that I ever saw,
   Coming for to carry me home,
   When Jesus washed my sins away,
   Coming for to carry me home.
   Chorus

4. I'm sometimes up and sometimes down,
   Coming for to carry me home,
   But still my soul feels heavenly bound,
   Coming for to carry me home.
   Chorus

The Drunken Sailor

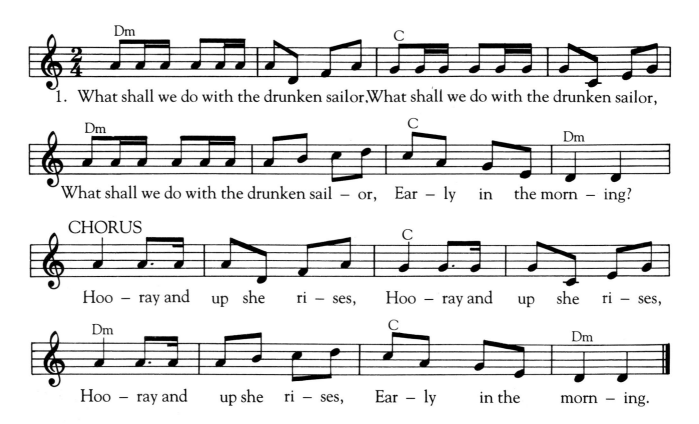

1. What shall we do with the drunken sailor, What shall we do with the drunken sailor,

What shall we do with the drunken sail – or, Ear – ly in the morn – ing?

CHORUS

Hoo – ray and up she ri – ses, Hoo – ray and up she ri – ses,

Hoo – ray and up she ri – ses, Ear – ly in the morn – ing.

2. Put him in the longboat till he's sober . . .
   Chorus

3. Hoist him aboard with a running bowline . . .
   Chorus

4. Put him in the scuppers with a hosepipe on him . . .
   Chorus

5. Pull out the plug and wet him all over . . .
   Chorus

6. Shave his belly with a rusty razor . . .
   Chorus

7. That's what we do with the drunken sailor . . .
   Chorus

Scarborough Fair

1. Are you going to Scar - bo - rough Fair? Pars - ley,

sage, rose - ma - ry and thyme.___ Re - mem - ber

me to one who lives there,_____

She once was a true love of mine._____

2. Tell her to make me a cambric shirt
   Parsley, sage, rosemary and thyme,
   Without any seam or needlework,
   Then she'll be a true love of mine.

3. Tell her to wash it in yonder dry well
   Parsley, sage, rosemary and thyme,
   Where water ne'er sprung, nor drop of rain fell,
   Then she'll be a true love of mine.

4. Tell her to dry it on yonder thorn
   Parsley, sage, rosemary and thyme,
   Which never bore blossom since Adam was born,
   Then she'll be a true love of mine.

5. Are you going to Scarborough Fair?
   Parsley, sage, rosemary and thyme.
   Remember me to one who lives there,
   She once was a true love of mine.

This Old Man

1. This old man, he played one, He played nick-nack on my drum;

CHORUS

Nick-nack, paddy whack, give a dog a bone, This old man came rol—ling home.

2. This old man, he played two,
   He played nick-nack on my shoe;
   Chorus

3. This old man, he played three,
   He played nick-nack on my tree;
   Chorus

4. This old man, he played four,
   He played nick-nack on my door;
   Chorus

26

5. This old man, he played five,
   He played nick-nack on my hive;
      Chorus

6. This old man, he played six,
   He played nick-nack on my sticks;
      Chorus

7. This old man, he played seven,
   He played nick-nack down in Devon;
      Chorus

8. This old man, he played eight,
   He played nick-nack on my gate;
      Chorus

9. This old man, he played nine,
   He played nick-nack on my line;
      Chorus

10. This old man, he played ten,
    He played nick-nack on my hen;
       Chorus

Pop Goes the Weasel

Up and down the Ci – ty Road, in and out the Ea – gle, That's the way the money goes,

Pop! goes the wea – sel.   Half a pound of tupp'ny   rice, half a pound of   trea – cle,

That's the   way the   mon – ey goes,   Pop!   goes the   wea – sel.

Sing a Song of Sixpence

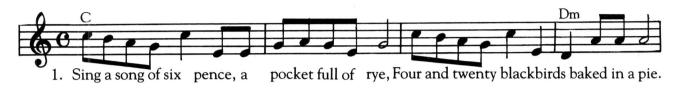

1. Sing a song of six pence, a pocket full of rye, Four and twenty blackbirds baked in a pie.

When the pie was opened the birds began to sing, Wasn't that a dainty dish to set before the King?

2. The King was in his counting-house, counting out his money,
   The Queen was in the parlour, eating bread and honey,
   The maid was in the garden, hanging out the clothes,
   When down came a blackbird, and pecked off her nose.

Lavender's Blue

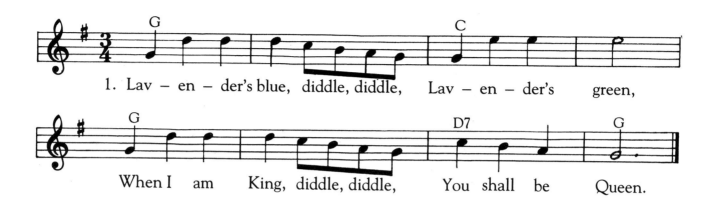

1. Lav – en – der's blue, diddle, diddle, Lav – en – der's green,
When I am King, diddle, diddle, You shall be Queen.

2. Call up your men, diddle, diddle,
Set them to work,
Some to the plough, diddle, diddle,
Some to the cart.

3. Some to make hay, diddle, diddle,
Some to cut corn,
While you and I, diddle, diddle,
Keep ourselves warm.

4. Lavender's green, diddle, diddle,
Lavender's blue,
If you love me, diddle, diddle,
I will love you.

Frère Jacques

Frè – re Jac – ques, Frè – re Jac – ques, Dor – mez vous? Dor – mez vous?

Son – nez les ma –ti – nes, son – nez les ma –ti – nes, Din din don, din din don.

Michael Finnigin

1. There was an old man called Michael Fin-ni-gin, He grew whiskers

on his chin-i-gin, The wind came up and blew them in-i-gin,

Poor old Mich-ael Fin-ni-gin. Be-gin-i-gin!

Last time: SHOUT

Fin-ni-gan, STOP

2. There was an old man called Michael Finnigin,
   He kicked up an awful dinigin,
   Because they said he must not sinigin,
   Poor old Michael Finnigin. Beginigin!

3. There was an old man called Michael Finnigin,
   He went fishing with a pinigin,
   Caught a fish but dropped it inigin,
   Poor old Michael Finnigin. Beginigin!

4. There was an old man called Michael Finnigin,
   Climbed a tree and barked his shinigin,
   Took off several yards of skinigin,
   Poor old Michael Finnigin. Beginigin!

4. There was an old man called Michael Finnigin,
   He grew fat and then grew thinigin,
   Then he died and had to beginigin,
   Poor old Michael Fin – ni – gin, STOP!

Oranges and Lemons

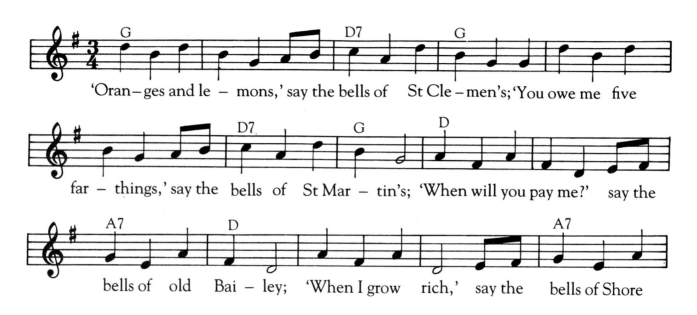

'Oran—ges and le — mons,' say the bells of St Cle—men's; 'You owe me five

far — things,' say the bells of St Mar — tin's; 'When will you pay me?' say the

bells of old Bai — ley; 'When I grow rich,' say the bells of Shore

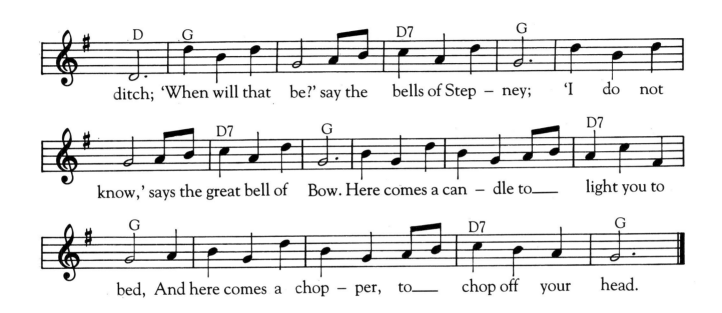

ditch; 'When will that be?' say the bells of Step – ney; 'I do not

know,' says the great bell of Bow. Here comes a can – dle to___ light you to

bed, And here comes a chop – per, to___ chop off your head.

One, Two, Three, Four, Five,

1. One, two, three, four, five, Once I caught a fish a – live,
Six, se – ven, eight, nine, ten, Then I let it go a – gain.

2. Why did you let it go?
   Because it bit my finger so.
   Which finger did it bite?
   This little finger on the right.

Here We Go Round the Mulberry Bush

1. Here we go round the mul – berry bush, the mul – berry bush, the mul – berry bush.

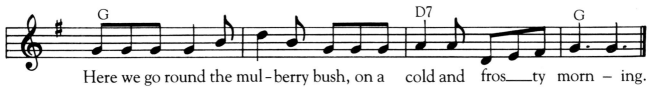

Here we go round the mul – berry bush, on a cold and fros___ty morn – ing.

2. This is the way we wash our hands . . .
3. This is the way we brush our hair . . .
4. This is the way we brush our clothes . . .
5. This is the way we go to school . . .
6. This is the way we come home from school . . .

37

Twinkle, Twinkle, Little Star

1. Twinkle, twinkle, little star, How I wonder what you are, Up above the world so high,

Like a diamond in the sky;____Twinkle, twinkle, little star, How I wonder what you are.

2. When the blazing sun is gone,
   When he nothing shines upon,
   Then you show your little light,
   Twinkle, twinkle, all the night.
   Twinkle, twinkle, little star,
   How I wonder what you are.

3. Then the traveller in the dark
   Thanks you for your tiny spark.
   Could he see which way to go
   If you did not twinkle so?
   Twinkle, twinkle, little star,
   How I wonder what you are.

4. In the dark blue sky you keep,
   And often through my curtains peep,
   For you never shut your eye
   Till the sun is in the sky.
   Twinkle, twinkle, little star,
   How I wonder what you are.

Click Go the Shears

1. Out on the board the   old shearer stands, Grasping his shears in his thin bony hands;

Fixed is his gaze on   a bare-bellied yoe   Glory if he gets her, won't he make the ringer go!

CHORUS

Click go the shears boys, click, click, click, Wide is his blow and his   hands move quick,   The

ringer looks around and is beaten by a blow, And curses the old snagger with the bare-bellied yoe.

2. In the middle of the floor in his cane-bottomed chair
   Sits the boss of the board with his eyes everywhere,
   Notes well each fleece as it comes to the screen,
   Paying strict attention that it's taken off clean.
   Chorus

3. The tar-boy is there waiting in demand
   With his blackened tar-pot, in his tarry hand,
   Spies one old sheep with a cut upon its back,
   Hears what he's waiting for, it's 'Tar here, Jack!'
   Chorus

4. Now the shearing is all over, we've all got our cheques
   So roll up your swags and it's off down the track.
   The first pub we come to it's there we'll have a spree,
   And everyone that comes along it's 'Have a drink with me'.
   Chorus

Greensleeves

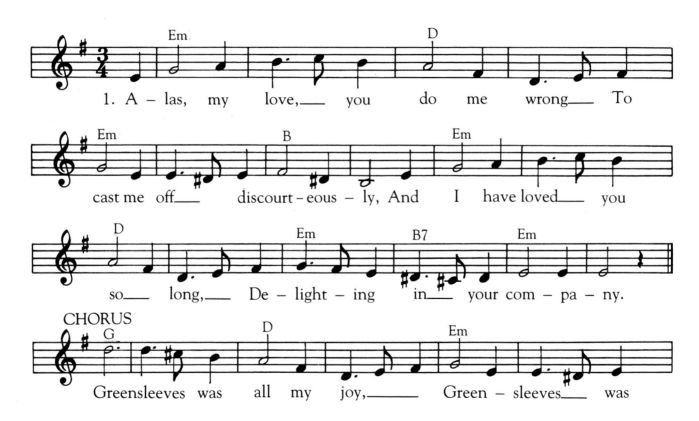

1. A – las, my love,___ you do me wrong___ To cast me off___ discourt - eous – ly, And I have loved___ you so___ long,___ De – light – ing in___ your com – pa – ny.

CHORUS

Greensleeves was all my joy,___ Green – sleeves___ was

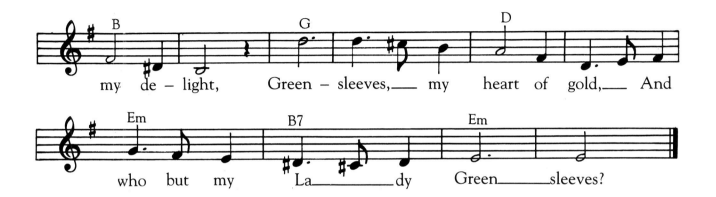

my de – light, Green – sleeves,___ my heart of gold,___ And

who but my La_____dy Green_____sleeves?

2. I have been ready at your hand
   To grant whatever you would crave,
   I have both waged life and land,
   Your love and goodwill for to have.
   Greensleeves was all my joy,
   Greensleeves was my delight,
   Greensleeves, my heart of gold,
   And who but my Lady Greensleeves?

The Skye Boat Song

2. Though the waves leap, soft shall ye sleep,
   Ocean's a royal bed.
   Rocked in the deep, Flora will keep
   Watch by your weary head.
   Chorus

3. Many's the lad fought on that day
   Well the claymore could wield.
   When the night came, silently lay
   Dead on Culloden's field.
   Chorus

4. Burned are our homes, exile and death
   Scatter the loyal men,
   Yet, e'er the sword cool in the sheath,
   Charlie will come again.
   Chorus

45

Billy Boy

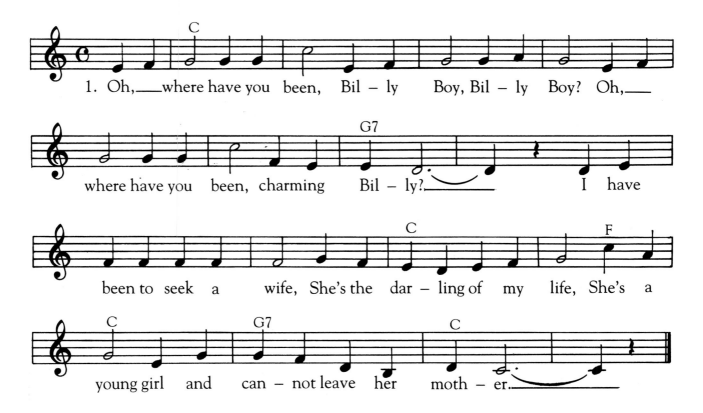

1. Oh,—where have you been, Bil – ly Boy, Bil – ly Boy? Oh,— where have you been, charming Bil – ly?— I have been to seek a wife, She's the dar – ling of my life, She's a young girl and can – not leave her moth – er.—

2. Did she bid you to come in, Billy Boy, Billy Boy?
   Did she bid you to come in, charming Billy?
   Yes, she bade me to come in,
   There's a dimple on her chin,
   She's a young girl and cannot leave her mother.

3. Can she bake a cherry pie, Billy Boy, Billy Boy?
   Can she bake a cherry pie, charming Billy?
   She can bake a cherry pie
   In the twinkling of an eye,
   She's a young girl and cannot leave her mother.